Praise for *Dear God*

I am not religious. This book should not be for me. But it was. Beautiful prose . . . brutal honesty . . . comfort and grace and relevance. Every moment I was reading it, I was not alone. What kind of magic is this?

JENNY LAWSON, *New York Times* bestselling
author of *Furiously Happy*

Already known for her hilarious storytelling, Bunmi Laditan returns with more of her humanity on display. Here she speaks with God honestly, giving us permission to do the same.

AUSTIN CHANNING BROWN, *New York Times*
bestselling author of *I'm Still Here*

Bunmi Laditan vulnerably and courageously shows us how to bring our doubts and accusations, our fears and uncertainties, to God directly. Bunmi opens her heart on every page, from the mundane to the deeply personal, as she blurs the lines between poetry and prayer, love and fear, trust and mistrust. If you've ever been afraid to bring your full self to God, ashamed that deep down you're not good enough for God to listen to, *Dear God* is a window into someone who has learned that faith isn't about trusting what we know but about trusting that we are known.

JARED BYAS, author of *Love Matters More* and
cohost of *The Bible for Normal People* podcast

Dear God

Dear God

HONEST PRAYERS

TO A GOD WHO LISTENS

Bunmi Laditan

ZONDERVAN BOOKS

ZONDERVAN BOOKS

Dear God
Copyright © 2021 by Bunmi Laditan

Requests for information should be addressed to:
Zondervan, *3900 Sparks Dr. SE, Grand Rapids, Michigan 49546*

Zondervan titles may be purchased in bulk for educational, business, fundraising, or sales promotional use. For information, please email SpecialMarkets@Zondervan.com.

ISBN 978-0-310-35918-0 (audio)

Library of Congress Cataloging-in-Publication Data

Names: Laditan, Bunmi, author.
Title: Dear God : honest prayers to a God who listens / Bunmi Laditan.
Description: Grand Rapids : Zondervan, 2020. | Summary: "This broken world so often breaks our hearts and sends us searching for a word of divine love. In Dear God, award-winning and beloved author Bunmi Laditan bravely says what we're all thinking in this wittingly fresh and stunningly relatable collection of letters drawn from her journey of prayerful wrestling with God"— Provided by publisher.
Identifiers: LCCN 2020023723 (print) | LCCN 2020023724 (ebook) | ISBN 9780310359166 (hardcover) | ISBN 9780310359173 (ebook)
Subjects: LCSH: Prayer—Christianity. | Presence of God.
Classification: LCC BV210.3 .L33 2020 (print) | LCC BV210.3 (ebook) | DDC 242—dc23
LC record available at https://lccn.loc.gov/2020023723
LC ebook record available at https://lccn.loc.gov/2020023724

Cover design: Thinkpen Design
Cover illustrations: Potapov Alexander / TairA / Shutterstock
Interior illustrations: Estee Zandee
Interior design: Denise Froehlich

Printed in the United States of America

20 21 22 23 24 25   /LSC/   10 9 8 7 6 5 4 3 2 1

To the God who sees me

I was raised in a religious household and around religious people, but can say in all truth that while religious ideas permeated my mind, they never touched my heart. I know there were some good people of faith around me, but I found myself fixating on the hypocrites, growing angry as I saw them flourish and their harmful actions go unchecked. I felt very little love in religious settings, only the weight of the cultural rules and disdain for those deemed as "outsiders" and "sinners." So I became one—an outsider. I wandered. I knew of God but had no relationship with God, and I felt a deep-down hatred for religious people—especially Christians, who I felt had repeatedly rejected and scorned me.

When I met and married a Jewish man, I was not required to convert to his faith, but I did. My upbringing had instilled in me the value of raising children in one faith tradition, and something about this people—who had been chased, hunted, all over the earth and yet still believed in God—spoke to me. I respected them. I wanted my children to learn their heritage of resilience in the face of extreme persecution. I wanted them to know the importance of *mitzvot* (good deeds), *tikkun olam* (repairing the world in any small way), and to be able to toast *l'chaim* (to life) even in difficult seasons.

So I studied. I forsook all past beliefs, shed the weight of my religious bitterness, and embraced the role of a Jewish mother. I was good at it. In fact, I loved it. Fridays were for kneading soft challah dough in my kitchen, my baby strapped to my back, sleeping against the rhythmic folding.

Saturdays were for rest and *shul* (synagogue), where I recited the *Shema* (a daily declaration of faith) and felt the power of the ancient prayer that calls all of Israel to set her sights on her Maker: "Hear, O Israel: The LORD our God, the LORD is one."*

I dutifully and joyfully signed up my oldest for Hebrew camp, decorated Chanukah cookies, dressed with *tzniut* (modesty), fasted on Yom Kippur, and studied Hebrew. I was content, happy in fact, in my new tribe.

When the marriage ended, however, I found myself floating. Suddenly the faith that had bound our family felt like a cruel joke.

I spent the next few years spiraling in and out of mental and emotional crises. I still occasionally baked challah, but never felt the same lightness of spirit when I did. I observed whatever holidays the culture around me deemed important, but I never prayed. Not even liturgical prayers.

Did I mention I was living in a new city, a new country, and barely knew a soul?

And yet something kept me afloat. I was always aware of a feeling of being seen and loved but didn't know where it came from. Luck? Karma? Nature? I didn't know.

A few years later, after having another child in a relationship that ended, I was once again on my own. Putting my hope in relationships hadn't worked. Putting my faith in every and any religion I could find—from paganism to multiple religions—had

---

* Deuteronomy 6:4.

worked for a while but ultimately left me feeling lost. So I decided to go to the Source.

I prayed. Wearing jeans and a hoodie, I approached the throne of a God I wasn't even sure existed and asked, "Who are you?"

And he answered.

Today, my Friday afternoons are filled with rushing to prepare for Shabbat, my three children giggling and playing as they anticipate their favorite day of the week—the one with no chores! My mind swirls with all the things I need to do: sweep the floors, make sure the *cholent* (stew) is going in the slow cooker so we have a warm meal on the one day I don't cook, and have the kids learn the *parsha* (weekly Bible portion). My mind is at peace. Not because I feel enveloped in the safety of a community or religion, but because I know *him*.

In my house, we call him *Yeshua*. You may know him as Jesus. To me, he's not a historical or political figure; he's my brother, friend, and literal savior.

I'm aware that, to many, my life may seem anything from strange to blasphemous. But if my *mashiach* (Messiah) observed Passover and kept Shabbat, I will too. One of the first things my God, whom I call Abba (father), reminded me of when I began to speak to him, was that he was there when I held the Torah in the synagogue during my conversion. He was there when I emerged from the warm waters of the *mikveh* (ceremonial bath).

It's only when I leave our cozy home that I sometimes feel as if I walk between two worlds—a mainstream Christian one with whom I share a Messiah, and a mainstream Jewish one with whom I share a painful history, daily life traditions, and relentless faith. It's not always easy, but I count myself blessed to finally know the peace that covers all circumstances.

If you'd have told me ten or twenty years ago that I'd say all this, I would have called you a liar. But all it takes is one encounter with the fisherman from a tiny, unimportant fishing village, a Messiah who loves like no one else, to be forever changed. It was through him that I finally and truly began to know God.

And the journey began.

Come along if you'd like.

Love, Bunmi

An angel once told me that things grow in the sun but are cured in the dark. Whether you are in a season of blooming or refining, my wish for you is peace.

Love,
ME

Dear God,

I was making a list of things I know for sure, but when I went to write "God loves me," I couldn't—it felt like a lie. I believe you love me, but I don't know it. I think you do. Your book says you do, but I guess in the back of my mind I see you as a giant Zeus—a despot in the sky. You knew Eve would eat the fruit. You created the tree. You allowed the Holocaust.

Have you heard the phrase, "With friends like you, who needs enemies?" I suppose that's why I find trusting you so hard. Jewish families in 1941 trusted you.

You said, "My ways are higher than your ways and my thoughts are higher than your thoughts,"* and I believe you, but I still brace myself for suffering I won't understand.

I believe you have a plan, but are you painting your masterpiece with my pain?

Love. I don't know what that means. I don't know that you love me, and I suppose I don't know if I love you either. I fear you and I respect your power, but I'm afraid your next move will take another chunk out of me.

What's love got to do with us?

Me

---

* See Isaiah 55:9.

DEAR GOD,

*I'm trying to stay hopeful, but doubt is my favorite food,
guilty displeasure, and holy water. It doesn't quite keep
me warm or satisfy my aching hunger for the feast of your
promises, but it's something. A meal of two steps backward.
Acidic punch. Empty. Never hydrates. Feed me.*

Love,
ME

DEAR GOD,

You sent your son to die to show your love. That's intense.
Van Gogh cut off his ear to show love.

Couldn't you have just restored the Garden of Eden?
Maybe put an electric fence around the tree?

Sometimes I think, If you'd let your son die, what will you
let happen to me, who is not a blood relative?

Your kind of love scares me.

ME

DEAR GOD,

Help me have the faith of a baby bird, a small child, an old woman. Speak to the fear in my soul so that it might recognize your voice, wake up, rise, thrive. Do something other than hide in the dark.

ME

DEAR GOD,

Sometimes, all the time, daily, every five minutes, I look at the world and know exactly why you flooded it.

ME

DEAR GOD,

You said, "I am with you always," and I assume you meant you are with me in spirit.

I believe you, but I need you to come down, from your holy hill, for a hug.

ME

DEAR GOD,

You know how when babies and toddlers fall asleep in the car and their heads flop down and to the side in a way that looks not only desperately uncomfortable but also like it's impossible to breathe? Do I ever look like that to you? Because that's how I feel. My life, my body, my everything needs adjusting so I can breathe again.

ME

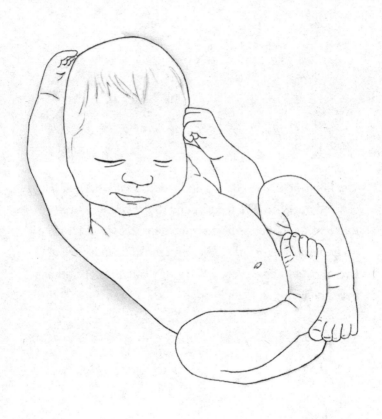

DEAR GOD,

I just thought about the verse that goes something like, "You formed me in my mother's womb."* Is that poetry or fact? It seems self-indulgent to imagine you both created the Milky Way and decided the length of my toenails, but I love the idea. If you were that close to the project that is me, as focused and intentional as Michelangelo sculpting the Pietà, maybe I could stop being so critical of every blemish and hair. I love thinking that you not only picked the exact shade of my skin from one cosmic paint strip, but also selected the pitch and cadence of my laugh and created the exact recipe for my smile. I can't hate myself if you did this.

Yours,

ME

---

* See Psalm 139:13.

DEAR GOD,

*I've messed up so badly. Made a real mess of things.
At times like this, I look at everyone I know with their
significantly neater, tidier lives and hate myself. I'm like
some kind of animal with no mouth and six legs that should
be put out of its misery. An abomination. I'm terrible at
being a fully grown human. You made me, and it's been
said you don't make mistakes. So explain it to me. Do I
have a purpose beyond dealing with administrative tasks
and obligations? Why am I here? I'm listening.*

That's what I thought.

ME

DEAR GOD,

After this life is all over, I have a fantasy about spending time alone with you amongst the stars, maybe sitting together in some black-glow nebula. Not talking much, just relaxing. Taking it all in. I'd be done asking for things, and you'd be done making life intentionally difficult. I want to enjoy you for once. Bask in your presence without needing a thing. Maybe you'd tell me some crazy stories. I know you've seen some stuff. I know there will be a long line of people more deserving than me of time alone with you, but please pencil me in. Anytime, really.

Love,
ME

DEAR GOD,

*I just want to say thanks for nature. I know we're
destroying it, and that must be pretty annoying, but it's
still very impressive. I'm sitting in my parked car (you can
probably see me) because I arrived early for something and
am looking at these gorgeous great big trees. I'm not hippie
enough to know the species, but their leaves look like giant
silver dollars. Some look lighter than others as the sun
streams through them. They flutter in the wind. You have
a tough reputation with all that fire and brimstone, but you
really are an artist. What's it like to be all things? Are you
ever at war with yourself?*

Love,
ME

Dear God,

Do you have a favorite name? What did you call yourself before you made us? What did you do before us? Do you have other humans somewhere? Are we Earth 6.0 or something? I honestly feel betrayed thinking about that. Is there some Earth elsewhere?

Me

PS. Do you like me? I know you love me, but do you like me?

Dear God,

Sometimes I put on sunglasses and stare directly into the sun, trying to understand you the way people who stare at paintings in museums are trying to understand exactly what the artist wanted the world to know about them. How they see the world. What their message was.

Mostly, I just get blind spots in my vision afterward. Is that your way of telling me to stop?

Me

Dear God,

Why did you make spiders? Were you mad? Did you think they were cute with all those legs? I respect you, but I don't think spiders were your best work. Unless you wanted us to live in fear, in which case, I say, "Mission accomplished."

Love,
Me

DEAR GOD,

Why can't butter be healthy? Are mushrooms really even food? Why didn't you make seedless pomegranates? You know we'd love that. It's like a puzzle. Isn't life hard enough? Why is the mango seed so big? Like, really big? It easily takes up half the mango. Is there a lesson in that? Like, for every mango in life, is there a big seed? Sorry, I'm hungry.

Love,
ME

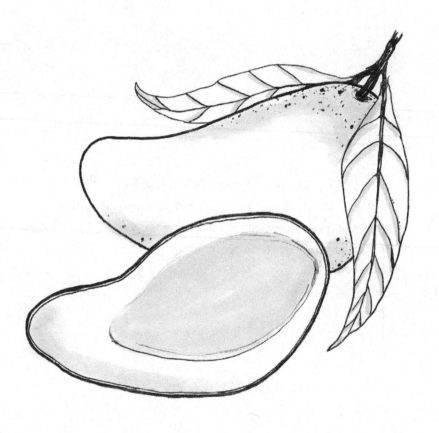

DEAR GOD,

Why don't you do more miracles? Okay, maybe you do tons of miracles all the time, but why not flashy ones where you take credit and sign "God Was Here" in the sky? I would do that, I think. So people would know. But you like to be subtle. Is it so that people have to look for you?

ME

DEAR GOD,

I decided not to believe in you. I was upset. Devastated,
actually. Tired of feeling like I'm speaking into empty air.
But that's not true. I can feel you almost all the time. I
was tired of being in pain. You could have rescued me if
you wanted to, but you didn't. That made me so sad. And
angry. So I renounced you in my soul and turned my back.
For three solid hours.

Did you miss me?

I'm still kind of mad.

ME

DEAR GOD,

I need money. Like thousands. I don't want to be rich; I just want to buy cheese without thinking about it. I know a lot of people have far less than me, so I don't want to press the issue, but I just bought gas and have only $25.38 to my name. But if you add in the debt I have, it's negative $8 million (rough estimate).

I'm eating today, so that's a step. But if you can please let me find pirate gold in a cave, that would be fantastic.

Love,
ME

Dear God,

Thank you for

good hugs
cups of tea
bonfires
the sound of rain
the kind of laughter that only gets more intense when you
    try to stop
brick walls
good graffiti
strangers with kind eyes
strangers who don't look at you when you're crying in public
quiet, deep people
loud, animated people
responsible people
messy people (Hi)
my bed
untouched snow
hoodies
buttered popcorn
crisp apples
iced coffee
fresh doughnuts
socks of all kinds
olive oil
distressed wood
blankets

Me

DEAR GOD,

*Some days, I'm so tired. Today was one of those days. I
slept okay. Ate normally (badly, but I'm used to it by now)
and had enough water (coffee, there's water in coffee).
It's a deep body fatigue, and I know where it comes from.
Some days, a lot of days, I carry around not only my body
but memories I'd like to forget. They stick to me like tar
and demand I watch a giant movie screen of my psyche
on repeat. They take human form and talk to me, God.
Interrogate me. Challenge my right to exist. Challenge me
to look in the mirror without deep shame.*

*Are these demons? Or are they a mixture—a soup of
memory and emotion come alive, powered by my fear?*

*Getting through these days is like walking with ankle
weights, wrist weights, a neck weight—you get the idea.*

*By sunset, my eyelids hang down, and I'm faking
everything. I've tried to banish these ghosts with drinks,
food, entertainment—nothing works the way talking to
you does. But sometimes I give in and become a willing,
desperate audience to their enactments of my worst
moments, their indictment of me.*

Make them stop.

Love,
ME

Dear God,

I woke up at 5:00 a.m., grateful you sent me back. I don't know what I was thinking. I wasn't thinking. I drove to the mountain in a daze of strange calm.

I still have a chance of getting this right. Every day hurts, but there are moments of peace where instead of rushing down rocky rapids, my boat floats, rocked tenderly by your hand. Am I okay?

Me

Dear God,

What was your objective when you made me? I mean, was I imbalanced at birth, or did a perfect storm of circumstance, environmental stressors, toxins from nonorganic apples, Tang, suspect lunch meat, and unclean spirits come together and mess up my brain? The highs are exhilarating—I believe I can fly and love everyone. The lows are a crawl toward the edge of a cliff where living in daily fear feels like my inevitable destiny. It's true that I've survived many battles at the edge of The End, but it only takes one time.

Life is gradually wearing at my hope, and with every battle barely won, I come out weaker.

Why am I like this? Someone who was born blind or without an appendage could ask the same question, I suppose, but going through life with your enemy lodged between your ears?

I'm tired.

I like to imagine the cracks in my mind let your light in better. Maybe my brokenness is like stained glass. Perhaps my brain is like a radio that can't tap into the Top 40 stations but plays a tune from heaven.

Maybe because I need more of you, you give more of yourself to me.

I don't know. I hope so.

Love,
Me

Dear God,

This broken, bloody world, my broken, bloody life. Is this your masterpiece? Are our tears and bones your mediums? How can I pretend you care about me in a world where innocents suffer? How can I pretend to matter? You don't know how badly I crave your attention, or maybe you do. I hate it here.

Love,
Me

Dear God,

I remember what it was like to float in the sky, free of a form pressed into human shape. No hands, no legs, no stomach, no eyes, yet I could see. Look down at my body. I looked like I was sleeping. Adorable. Like a baby, curled up. I don't know why you sent me back, but you could have at least said hello first.

Me

DEAR GOD,

Assuming I get to heaven, I don't want neighbors.

ME

DEAR GOD,

I asked for forgiveness today. Please help me to be
harmless. Soften my broken parts so they don't cut those
around me. The closest ones are the most vulnerable.
Make me a dove.

Love,
ME

DEAR GOD,

Forgiving someone who isn't sorry feels like washing a car that isn't mine. Why should I do it? Because you forgive me over and over? You're literally God though. I'm a trash human. Please help me forgive. If only because the anger is slowly but surely choking me.

ME

DEAR GOD,

I want to be a better person, but sometimes the past feels more real than the present or even the future. How do I move on from who I've been to who I want to be? I hope heaven is nice today. It sucks down here, as usual.

Love,
ME

DEAR GOD,

I imagine your grace to be like an "it's okay" cloud of forgiveness. I don't do anything perfectly, but the grace says, "It's okay," and knows I'm trying. I really am trying. I know I mess up a lot and blame you for my mistakes, but I'm trying to grow. I find it hard to believe you can love someone like me. I haven't killed anyone—yet (joke), but I don't keep my promises to you. I forget what you tell me, and it's obvious I don't fully trust you. Maybe if you weren't so invisible, this would be easier. Have you thought of not being invisible? I'd love to hold your hand.

Love,
ME

DEAR GOD,

I've started smoking again. I know your spirit lives within me, so I apologize. I'm a terrible host.

Love,
ME

DEAR GOD,

I feel like we're playing chess. I make a move, then you make a move. Except we're in the dark. And I'm crying. Other than that, this is fun.

ME

DEAR GOD,

I feel so alone. This must be getting old for you. It's getting old for me. I'd love to leave this place but can't do that without hurting the people who depend on me. I'll say it because you already know I think it—I wish I hadn't been born. This is a ride I never would have gotten on if I'd known. And I was foolish enough to bring other people on it. It's my greatest fear that one day they'll feel the way I do, live the way I do—smiling in public while dying, withering on the inside.

I pray often. Send SOS smoke signals to you, the angels, anyone who can hear.

Please come get me. Please come get all of us. I can't be the only one who feels like this. I'm not dead, but I'm not alive. Every breath hurts.

ME

Dear God,

*I can't shake the feeling that you're deeply disappointed
in everything I do. And that I'm messing up almost every
moment of the day. Help me to feel like your child and not
like your Worst Employee of the Month.*

Love,
Me

DEAR GOD,

Why do you hide? Is it because you want me to seek? I'm tired. And lost. And tired. Come out.

Love,
ME

DEAR GOD,

I'm not trying to tell you how to do your job, but I think dogs should talk.

Love,
ME

DEAR GOD,

Caterpillars are gross. Butterflies are beautiful. I see what you did there.

Love,
ME

Dear God,

The only thing getting me through this is knowing, hoping, that one day, I and all the people I love will be where you are.

I'm not okay down here.

Love,
Me

Dear God,

Hope is a dangerous thing to have. Every time I feel a spark of it trying to light the dark places in my heart, I blow it out. No more, I tell myself and return to the gray. I've tried hope before, believed in my good dreams, thought, Today will be the day, and each time I was wrong. Each time I thought I heard you, I was wrong. Hope tells me about things I can't have and realities that will never be mine. This is my life, this will always be my life, this has always been my life—I'll always either feel alone or be alone. The sooner I accept it, the sooner things will get easier. Hope is not for me. Please stop trying.

Love,
Me

DEAR GOD,

You know how much we need you—a Father who loves us—but you hide behind layers and layers of veils and clouds. You left us one long letter written in ancient languages and haven't written since . . . nothing clear anyway. Nothing decipherable. Just dreams and whispers. We can't live on dreams and whispers, not when everything is so loud. I hope heaven is nice today. You have kids here.

Love,
ME

DEAR GOD,

I know you do a lot. They say you hold the atmosphere together with your hands and command the sun to rise each morning. You know what I'd trade for all of that? Knowing without a doubt that you care. Drop the atmosphere and hold me.

ME

DEAR GOD,

I'm tired of the signs. At some point on the journey they feel mocking. I drove in circles today, lost, for almost an hour. It felt so self-referential. I couldn't find the way, even amongst familiar roads. There was so much construction that my GPS didn't know either. Neither of us knew. I don't know how I got out of it. I'd like to think it was you, but even a broken clock is right twice a day. These days, I wish I didn't believe. It's less painful thinking you don't exist than thinking you do and you're just watching me wander. Hope you're good.

ME

Dear God,

In heaven, if I get there, I'm most looking forward to being
alone in peace. No one to worry about, no one who can
hurt me, no goals to reach, no pressure, no longing, no
wondering why, no pain, nothing. Just quiet. I'd love a
cottage in the farthest corner, away from all the noise.
You can visit anytime, but don't bring anyone. Maybe
Saturday nights we can play a board game or just talk for
a few minutes. I know you'll have a busy schedule. Even
once a month or every few months would work. Whatever
you can schedule. I'll find ways to occupy myself. Reading
mostly and walks. The same as here.

Love,
Me

DEAR GOD,

You saved me. You've saved me more than once, and I don't know why. I go back and forth between gratitude and sadness. The pain could've been over, but it would have just begun—like the worst baton pass of all time—for the ones I love the most. So I'm here. Why me? There have been so many others you didn't save, whose souls you didn't give another chance, so why me?

A blanket of thankfulness and nothingness is draped over me. Nothing feels right. You brought me back, but where are you? I'm alone.

ME

Dear God,

*I don't blame you for any of this. I see how I created my
life and set myself up for failure. It wasn't intentional.
It's because I believed I could be something I've always
known deep down I couldn't. I've always known there
was something wrong with me but thought I could put on
a cloak of normalcy and pass. Pass I did not. It's almost
funny. The most painful part isn't feeling separated from
other people but being separated from you. I lost my taste
for this world a long time ago. I'm not afraid of death. I
no longer believe anyone's coming to help—that was my
biggest weakness, believing someone could or would come
and make everything okay. No one is coming, and even
if someone did, they'd only make it worse in the end. I
learned that the hard way. I'm just waiting. Handling my
obligations and waiting. It's not all bad. It's a privilege to
love my family, but I know I'm not home.*

Anyway, I hope you're well. I wish you'd write back.

Me

DEAR GOD,

I asked for help. I reached out and told the truth, and someone was there. Is that why you created Eve? You knew humans were no good left talking only to animals and plants? That we'd need another to hold the candle when ours goes out? Thank you. I don't know if my faith has been restored, but at least I remember what it's like to believe. I feel a warmth that wasn't there before.

ME

When I walk through the valley of the shadow of death,
  you are there.
When I dance in the meadows of life's delirious joys,
  you are there.
When I wander the dense forests of confusion,
  you are there.
While I climb, weary, up the mountain of my daily
  responsibilities,
unrelenting chores,
and demands of my spirit,
  you are there.
When at the end of the day
I sit by your still waters,
my mind cooled by the clear singing streams,
  you are there.
Peace and gratitude rise in me,
morning rays across a purple waking sky,
because I know
  you are there.

DEAR GOD,

It's official. I've lost the will to help myself. I've lost the will to save myself. You're the only one who can do it now.

Love,
ME

Dear God,

*I'm trying to quit some of the bad habits I know you hate,
but . . . how do I say this . . . I need them. This world is
cold, and my vices keep me somewhat warm. I don't know
how else to say it. I'm not going to lie to you. I want to be
the best version of me for you, but this is all I can do for
now. I know there will be consequences, and I pray daily
for a grace I know I don't deserve.*

Love,
Me

DEAR GOD,

I long for a life that I love, but I'm scared because heaven has been something I've been looking forward to for so long. I don't know what it's like to fear death. I only know what it's like to fear life. I've only ever seen this place as hell on a breezy day. Maybe, deep down, I prefer it this way.

I don't know, God. Things have been so hard for so long, I've begun to believe that struggle is who I am, not what I've experienced. Somewhere along the line, I began to believe that being happy isn't a possibility for me. At this point, I'm afraid to like it here because I know everything in this life is temporary. How can it be worth it to love life when it could slip away at any moment?

I'm not sure I want to get attached.

But I do want to be happy . . . I think.

Hope you're well.

ME

DEAR GOD,

I don't know if I love you. I respect you. I understand you're in charge. I capitalize in all of the right places out of deference, but I don't know you as a Father—more as a distant king. Even after the miracles, something is missing. I can't manage to stay close to you. Either you're slippery or I'm bad at holding things, but I feel like you're a million miles away.

Anyway, just wanted to be honest.

ME

Dear God,

I shoveled my elderly neighbor's stoop this morning. He
was angry that a closer neighbor, one he shares a porch
with, never does his side. I shoveled the other neighbor's
side too, and it made the elderly neighbor angry. He said
his neighbor didn't deserve it. I told him nobody deserves
anything. And I meant it. I get his anger. I do. But if we
all treated people according to what they deserved, I think
we'd all be in hell. And we are, to some extent. Better to
just do things for you. That's what I told him when he said
I was a nice person. That I was doing it for you.

To be honest, I don't like either of the neighbors, so it's true.

Hope you're good.

Me

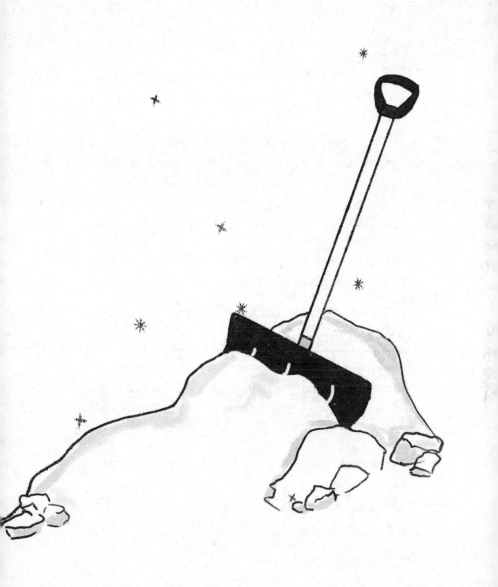

Dear God,

I've been thinking about forgiveness a lot lately. You've seen into my heart. You know what I keep in there and that bitterness, anger, and hurt drip from the walls like sticky honey.

I've tried to forgive and let go, but just when I think I'm over it, something will remind me—and it's like I'm living in a nightmare again.

Is it possible to forgive and forget, or is forgiveness simply a decision to try?

I want to forgive the way you say you do—removing all memory of sin and shame, throwing them as far as the east is from the west,* wiping the slate clean, but I'm not God. I'm me.

Forgiving. How do I do this? How do I do it when letting go might leave me vulnerable to being hurt again? How do I do it when the person isn't even sorry?

---

* See Psalm 103:12.

When the anger comes back, I choose to try to forgive,
because you forgave me. If I believe in your forgiveness, I
have to believe in mine too.

The power to forgive must be the strongest in the universe.
It's a legacy that comes from you. Help me be powerful
enough to let things go. Help me, God, because I can't do
it by myself. I want so badly to forgive, not for their sake,
but for mine, because the burden of the past is too heavy to
carry into each new day.

Help me, God.

Love,
ME

Dear God,

People don't really believe in you anymore, and can you blame them? I mean, look at the world. If my house were a mess, the door hanging off the hinges and windows all busted out with wind whipping through them, no one would believe I was home. That's what the world looks like.

Yes, miracles happen. They seem to be your calling card, but you don't sign them. Unlike terrorists who are quick to take credit for their atrocities, you operate in silence and in the dark.

Why not be obvious, like in the days of Judah?

But I guess even the children of Israel were quick to forget you as they wandered the desert. They were quick to complain and be afraid, even as your cloud guided them by day and fire by night.

No matter how close you are, we doubt, it seems. We're hopeless in all definitions of the word.

It seems to be our birthright to doubt and yours to forgive it, over and over again. Even if you were as clear as the hand in front of my face, it wouldn't matter. As long as there is a shred of separation between us, we will feel utterly lost. As long as there is a gap as wide as a hair between us, we will cry.

My heart longs for the day my soul returns to yours.

Until then.

Love,
ME

DEAR GOD,

Thanks for coffee. That is all.

Love,
ME

DEAR GOD,

How did you think of clouds?

ME

Dear God,

Does heaven watch us on TV? Is earth reality television for heavenly hosts and departed souls? Am I on basic cable, or is my life a premium channel? Please tell my viewers I'm sorry for the swearing (are you bleeping it out?).

Love,
Me

DEAR GOD,

An angel told me alcohol isn't always a problem, but I should be careful what I'm drinking to. Sometimes I toast my pain.

ME

DEAR GOD,

I can feel your compassion surrounding me. In these moments when I feel your gentle eye on me, I know you're my father, and I'm not afraid. Stay.

ME

Dear God,

Deliver me. Be my midwife, and deliver my body and soul from this working turmoil. Let me be birthed, anew, into the land you whispered into my soul through my dreams all those months ago. Deliver me. Let me take my first breath of cool air.

Love,
Me

DEAR GOD,

I've tasted the sweet, vanilla-scented perfume of your presence. One day I'll be enveloped in the sweet mist of you. My home. Until then, stay close. Don't leave me or blink. I don't know if you've noticed, but I have a tendency to get into trouble.

Love,
ME

I know where my love ends,
I've felt it run out.
Weary evenings after exhausting workdays and long
    commutes
turn into sharp words and spit-out sentences.
Furrowed eyebrows and pursed lips
replace the gentle eyes and soft kisses of morning
because my love ran out.
But you, O God—
I haven't found the place your love runs out.
I've searched in the valley of disobedience
and found the pain of correction,
but your warm embrace was also there.
I ventured to the peaks of rebellion and
tumbled down, hitting every hard rock,
landing on the back of a waiting eagle,
who flew my bloodstained, heart-shamed, tattered self
    to a nest
where I recovered.
In the depths of my despair, I turned my back to you,
falling into the void of nothing,
choosing emptiness and echoes of my own thoughts to
    yours,
and you sent angels
with food, pillows, and grace
to guide me out of the cave.
Now I'm older. Tired. No longer an explorer
but a child again at last,
content to warm myself against the fires of your heart
and marveling at a love
that has no end.

Dear God,

Hope is a funny thing. Just when you think it'll be winter forever, the snow begins to melt and ice-cold rivulets of fresh water trickle down the paths formed by salty tears. Icicles crack and groan before tumbling to the ground. And somewhere in the center of a white, frost-covered meadow, a single green baby sapling rises.

Me

Dear God,

Your angels say, "Fear not," so many times, but I'm afraid.
Not because an angry pharaoh is chasing me through a
desert, but because I can't see the plan. I am confident you
have one. I believe you do. But I have not been "cc'd" on
the document. I have not been patched into the conference
call. I was not consulted on the project.

I'm in the dark on everything but your promises and your
nature—both good. Is that how you want it? It must be.

I don't know how we're getting from point A to point B,
and I'm afraid it will hurt.

Our relationship was forged in my struggle, but is that
where it will live?

Please help me taste something other than fear. Surely
there is more to life. Am I blind to it? Help me to learn a
language other than pain. Help me to not be afraid.

Love,
Me

Dear God,

My plan is to hide within your heart for life. I know that whatever happens, whatever spring arrives or dawn breaks, nothing will calm my spirit like yours. My soul finds rest only in your presence, and my healing begins only in your living waters.

Whatever happiness or joy I taste in this world, nothing can or has come close to the precious moments I've spent in silence with you. I've heard your voice, and it lives, echoing within the chambers of my consciousness. I crave more and feel heaven in my midst when I pray.

Stay close to me, reveal your secrets and keep me as a child and friend.

Stay near is all I ask.

Love,
Me

DEAR GOD,

Sometimes faith is like hiking up a mountain, and other days it's the slide down. Today it's the latter, and I'm enjoying the breeze on my face.

ME

Dear God,

I never liked to worship. All that hands-up and eyes-closed stuff really freaks me out for some reason. It looks a little culty. I knew if anyone deserves praise it's you, but the idea that you're a king in need of adoration—some Henry IV in the sky—seemed unbecoming. And you know how I feel about authority in general.

But then I went through the valley of the shadow of death. All around me, shadows and demons loomed. I could hear their snapping teeth and see the glint of their eyes. They drew my blood and scorched my soul. I needed you—all the time—just to be okay. I needed the voice of saints more confident than me in my ear, reminding me of who you are and how you love and how you protect and how you promise and how your promises do not fail. I needed it twenty-four hours a day while my eyes were open and while they were closed and my mind raged on in the depths of my subconscious.

Lord God, I needed the praise. Worship became my refuge. In it, I found you not basking but smiling at the melodic affirmations of the love you have for your children.

It wasn't about ego. You have no ego. Worship is automatic in your presence because your being is worthy and deserving.

One day, I found victory after repenting of the last few strands of lies binding my heart, covering my mouth, and praise burst out, not as a response to a catchy tune, but as a tear-soaked, sobbing, and joyful song.

My lungs, mouth, and lips became a musical instrument. The song was written by another but was drenched in my story, which hung on each note. It was a story of a child who was lost and then was found, and the One who loves. The One who never gives up.

I worshiped. In traffic. I probably looked like a lunatic. But who cares when all of heaven is singing with you?

If I have one wish now, it's that every broken heart knew that the love they're aching for is so close—

so real,

alive and faithful,

and all you want is their yes,

all you want is their heart.

Love,
ME

DEAR GOD,

You taught me about agreements today as we walked through our special garden.

You taught me how the motivation behind every action is either faith or fear. You taught me that when I make a decision out of fear, I come into agreement with it and hand over my authority to it. I sublease my scepter to fear. I give it power of attorney.

But when I pause, remember who you are and who I am in you, and affirm myself as your child, miracles and blessings can be released into my life because I have not donated my crown to a lesser, undeserving power.

Thank you for being my teacher.

Did I get an A? If so, please put this on your fridge. Somewhere near the middle, please.

Love,
ME

DEAR GOD,

*I didn't love you because I confused you for your children
on their worst days and equated you with buildings.*

You are so much more.

Love,
ME

DEAR GOD,

Do you sing, or am I your song?

Love,
ME

Dear God,

Thank you for loving me the way I've always wanted to be loved.

Me

Dear God,

Your face chases my shadows away, and your voice rewrites my story.

Me

DEAR GOD,

Do you cry? Jesus did. He cried when Lazarus died, even though he knew resurrection was coming. It hurt. Do you cry? You created crying—rivers summoned by pain, blurred vision, the washing of cheeks with sorrow. Do you cry?

Love,
ME

DEAR GOD,

I've prayed for this so long and hard. I'm loosening my grip, resting on the promise, closing my tired eyes, and floating in the cloud made of my prayers, a blanket of pleas, lifting me up toward you.

Love,
ME

When fear demands my audience,
with its urgent whispers,
cold hands grasping at my temples,
racing toward my heart like wild ivy,
help me to breathe,
stay in your unmoving presence,
keep my eyes fixed on your throne
and my mind on your holy hill.
It's you who holds my future,
writes my days, and covers my nights.
Stay close to me, please,
now and forevermore.
Amen.

Dear God,

Thank you for showing me how to forgive. The deep caves of jagged rock where I hide my wounds are not too dirty for your presence.

I didn't want you to see what I keep in those shrouded
        places,
afraid you'd be repulsed by my bitter secrets
and dumpsters of pain piled high and rotting,
but your waters flowed there,
washing over my infected wounds.
I was afraid,
but the waters continued to flow
until it was finished
and I was new.

Love,
ME

DEAR GOD,

One day, we will meet. I know it. We've been through too
much not to. Even if it's just to tell me that I was so close
to heaven but, unfortunately, it's full. What I'm looking
forward to more than anything else in the world, the
moment I daydream about, the one that makes my heart go
warm and my breath short, is to hug you—to be wrapped
in your arms of light, feeling your complete love, bathing
in your presence, and knowing, without a doubt, that I'm
home. Even for a little while.

Love,
ME

DEAR GOD,

Your glory, a cloud of thin white fog,
surrounds me and my heart leaps
over and over
as a new song belts in the chambers of my soul,
which dances for joy at your presence.
You reward those who seek you hungrily in the dark,
who cry out
and scream for you,
rage at you.
You reward us with
joy untold
joy unheard
joy unleashed.
You are the King of kings and Lord of worlds,
and I, your little child,
delight in your smile
and bask in the glory of your name.

Love,
ME

DEAR GOD,

My words fail me
as I lie in the warm heart of your love,
your pristine beach of crystal,
defying winter,
erasing doubt,
canceling shame.
A taste of heaven.

Love,
ME

Dear God,

My soul recognizes the scent of your presence
and cries out at the voice of its Father.
Your scent
is in the wind,
and my soul rises.
My arms rise,
held up by angels.
I am enraptured.

Me

DEAR GOD,

How did I doubt? How did I question?
In the midst of your presence,
your glory heals
and restores every crack.
My brokenness evaporates,
and the entirety of my being screams in joy,
for you are here.

Love,
ME

DEAR GOD,

> Prince of peace
> King of joy
> Love embodied
> How do I describe the beginning and the end?
> All that is
> unencumbered by definition—
> glory,
> majesty,
> mercy.
> My Father,
> I am undone.

Love,
ME

DEAR GOD,

I am quite sure
I will never know the depths of your love for me,
so I say,
Thank you, Father,
I am
yours
forever.

Love,
ME

Dear God,

When they ask me how I know who you are, what do I say?
How do I describe what you do to my heart?
How do I describe the winds of your voice against my neck?
How do I explain how my spirit leaps for joy at your name?
How you've held me?
How I fell,
tumbled so far,
and you caught me
in those hands?
How do I describe our song?
How?
How can words capture you?
How can the creation capture the Creator?
They chase and grasp.
The only thing I can do is let them see my heart
and what you have done to it.
My Father,
our Father,
All There Is,
Love,
Lord Almighty,
my Friend,
my Redeemer,
I love you.

Me

DEAR GOD,

> You stand just out of reach
> and let me chase you,
> my hands catching the tip
> of your flowing garment
> before you laugh and run faster.
> I laugh, and my lungs pump as I run faster,
> you staying just out of reach,
> then slowing down,
> letting your glory graze my soul
> before running out of reach again.
> I will never stop chasing
> as you lead me closer
> and closer
> to your heart,
> my only home.

Love,
ME

DEAR GOD,

Life has a way of making us feel worthless. The dust collected over time, the shame. Some days I don't feel human; I feel like a wounded animal. I know that's not what you called me to be, and I know that's not my identity in you, so why do I feel this way? Is it because my pain is louder than your promises in my heart? I know I don't have your love because I deserve it but because I'm yours, but this free gift, while easy to unwrap, is hard to put on. It makes everything else in my closet look old. I don't feel like the person you say I am.

They call this imposter syndrome, but it's more than that. I keep picking up the past you've told me to put down. Like Hosea's wife, I can't accept my new station or last name. The slums know me, and I know them.

Help me find belonging in you. Help me find rest.

Love,
ME

Jonah prayed from inside the fish,
from the depths of the depths,
a man known for running,
fleeing,
while in the innards of the beast,
already consumed,
feasted on.
He prayed,
"Yet I will look again toward your holy temple."*
With all signs of hope gone,
his body a finished meal,
he turned to you
and believed.

---

* Jonah 2:4.

Dear God,

I'm not listening today. I'm being stubborn, and I know it. I'm tired of doing the right thing. What's the point? No one else does. Everyone just does what they want. I'm tired of trying so hard to stay in your lane when I can't even see your taillights. I'm tired. Just let me fail. Let me go. Give up on me.

Me

DEAR GOD,

I know I'm not from here. I'm a citizen of a place I can't remember but yearn for. What would you have me do here? Tell me so I can finish my project quickly. Every night I dream of being in a place that feels like home. I lie in bed and dream of looking around and saying in my heart, "Yes, this is right."

Until then,

ME

DEAR GOD,

*Does one need to forget to forgive? It seems like only you
should do that. You can't get caught off guard, but we
can. So we stay hardened and keep our eyes open. But
one always finds what they're looking for, so how can we
forgive without forgetting? Give me the grace to forgive like
you, even though I lack your strength and foresight.*

*Help me to be strong enough to let go of what's hurting me
to hold on to you.*

Love,
ME

DEAR GOD,

*Help me gently quit the habits I picked up out of despair.
Heal my heart, mind, and body. They're both broken and,
I fear, diseased. Only you can heal me now.*

Love,
ME

DEAR GOD,

Heal me from this spirit of criticism. Heal me from seeing problems and lies in everything. It's a filter I learned at some point—through bitterness, I suspect. I trust nothing. It's an angry way to look at life. It's violent. It's prideful and wrong. Help me to look at others with love. Help me to see people as you see them. Soften my gaze. I'm in no place to judge, and I know it. Give me humble eyes and a soft heart.

Love,
ME

DEAR GOD,

They say hurt people hurt people. Cover my brokenness with a blanket of your grace. Sand down my sharp edges with your gentle words. Let me leave no marks or bruises on any of your children, and if I do, please extend your healing to them swiftly. Let my mouth speak only words of peace.

Love,
ME

Dear God,

You weave miracles seamlessly into the tapestry of my life, not wishing to be obvious but desiring to be savored as I wonder, Could it be . . .? Was that . . . ? You leave the lightest of footprints, ones that are so easily blown away by the wind but never seem to disappear completely. Your ways are subtle and extravagant all at once. So easily taken for granted, if one wishes, but if one wishes, they could also stand in awe. Your masterpiece shifts according to the heart of the viewer; it is moved and unmoving.

Your word sits on the page, yet it is alive, and once planted in the right soil, in a chosen heart, it turns and grows like a child in a womb. Everything you do, everything you speak, your breath, contains life.

I ask that you speak your living words over me and mine.

Love,
Me

You weave my destiny together,
and I sit here pulling threads,
criticizing colors,
weeping over last year's patches,
fretting over tomorrow's patterns,
screaming as we sit too close to the fire.
God, please push your loom back,
lest I go up in flames,
my quilt reduced to smoke and gaudy ash.
You look up from your work and smile,
your hands still moving so fast they're a blur,
and pull an edge of coverlet over my trembling form
and hum me to sleep.

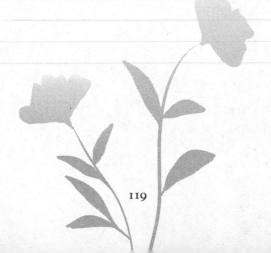

DEAR GOD,

What was it like in heaven today? How did the crystal lake
shimmer and shine? Was the angel choir as glorious as I
know it was? How did the new souls burst into praise when
they broke through the clouds? Tell me about the eyes of
the saints. What gifts did you give? As proud as I hope to
make you with my time here, I long to be home and in the
peace of your grace and glory. But not yet. Let my arrival
be so well-timed that at my passing, the tears of those I love
come from hearts at peace. Let them say I lived a good life
for you, long enough for me to spin a garment of loving
memories to keep them warm until we're together again.

Let it be like that.

How is heaven today?

Did you think of me?

I thought of you.

Love,
ME

DEAR GOD,

Any identity I've claimed or worn that is false, any mask
I've molded to fit over my face, I ask you today to burn it.

Love,
ME

DEAR GOD,

In my dream, you, like a pickaxe, smashed through my heart of concrete. When the rubble was gone, cleared and swept away, you laid down soft soil. You watered it and planted a garden in the hole in my chest. It flourished. Where there was once stone, life flourished.

Let it be.

Love,
ME

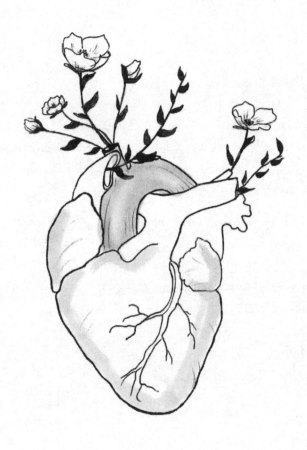

Dear God,

Align my feelings with your promises. Remind me to whisper your soothing lullabies to my heart when the waves crash and the thunder cracks, not so I fall asleep but so I can rest in your strength.

Help me honor you with my emotions. As you train me to raise my voice above the storm, gird my loins and do not let my foot be moved.* Meet me on the rock, surrounded by rising waters, and lift me above the illusion of death into life everlasting.**

Love,
Me

---

*   See Psalm 121:3.
** See Psalm 61:2; 18:16.

DEAR GOD,

Each time I've tried to lead my life I've steered it onto the rocks. As I sort through the rubble again, examining the tattered remains of my misplaced pride, I am both tired and grateful that you loved me enough to never let me make my home anywhere but in your heart. I ignored the whispers, so you shouted in the wind and your voice tore through my sails.

I mend them together now, slowly and deliberately, making sure each stitch bears your name.

I am royalty through you. Let me never wave a beggar's flag again. I am chosen. Let me never speak the language of the orphan. I am provided for. Let me never make a meal of scraps.

Love,
ME

DEAR GOD,

So much of what I hate about myself is a counterfeit painting, one that resembles me but is not me, a portrait commissioned by the enemy. Help me to decipher lies about who I am when they drift by so I can avoid the temptation to reach out my hand and claim them once again.

I am not who the enemy says I am. I am who you say I am, and you have called me yours.

You have called me yours. You have erased yesterday. You forgive freely and only want me to grow. The enemy wants me to drown in the stagnant waters of my past and call it swimming.

Help me to remember who you say I am. Help me to remember your brushstrokes on my face.

I am yours.

Love,
ME

Dear God,

Just when the enemy thought he had me,
when the world said I was done,
when the audience's laughter reached fever pitch,
when I was done,
when I was finished,
when my story was over,
you said no
and silenced all of hell with one word.
My eyes opened,
my heart took an unearned beat,
my lungs filled with new air,
and my soul returned.

Love,
Me

Dear God,

I won't lie. I'm afraid. I know the plans you have for me are good, but I know the fickle nature of my heart, and my head does nothing better than create nightmares out of shadows.

I'm afraid, but I'm standing,
sword in hand,
song in my heart,
angels at my left and right,
eyes open,
heart full of your word,
mouth full of your breath.
Praise will be the stones
launched at Goliath,
and when we win,
there will be no doubt
you were there.

Love,
ME

DEAR GOD,

Let not my brothers and sisters be casualties of the battle.
They're not my flesh and blood, no,
we're closer than that.
We have the same Father;
our souls were born in the womb of the Divine,
side by side,
separated by buildings and theology,
but one in the Lamb.
Rescue my sisters and my brothers,
hear their cries.
Let their faces fall softly on my heart,
let me hear their cries,
let them not be casualties of my pride
and my illegitimate attachment to this place.
Remind me they are all that matters;
after you, they are all that matters,
my brothers and sisters.

Love,
ME

DEAR GOD,

I learned that on the days my past demands my present
and brings with it shame, anger, and self-pity,
on the days I disconnect from you
and tune into hell's frequency
and begin to dance to the enemy's delight,
the way back to you
is praise,
psalms uttered urgently to myself while the thunder roars.
In the beginning, it falls like rain on a well-thatched roof,
but after a while,
one by one,
drops begin to penetrate my broken heart,
and as I remember who you are,
I remember who I am.
Let me remain here forever.

Love,
ME

Dear God,

Thank you for ripping my wounds open.
They were infected,
sealed with jagged stitches,
and you sliced them,
letting the rot see light,
and cleansed them,
letting your living waters,
your healing streams, run down.
I screamed,
screamed at the pain,
blamed you for it all,
and when the rivers ran clear,
you put me back together,
stitch by careful stitch
as I sobbed into your robes
until I fell asleep.
Thank you.

Me

DEAR GOD,

Teach me to stop acting and thinking like an orphan. No matter who calls me theirs on this earth, I have a Father and a home in heavenly places. I am not an orphan. I am held in your strong and loving embrace through every step and every breath. I am not an orphan. I am your child and was your child before my eyes opened in this place. Don't let me forget, Father, that I am not an orphan.

I am yours.

ME

Dear God,

You've taught me that impatience is disbelief in work-clothes. Help me to wait. I get afraid and make hasty plans that cause me so much pain and take so much time for me to untangle myself from. Help me to trust you, talk to you, to sit on my hands and wait. You're teaching me patience, and it burns. As my disbelief smolders into ash, pour your cooling grace on me.

Hum a song for me, please, as I wait.

Love,
Me

DEAR GOD,

You give good gifts. That is all. Thank you.

Love,
ME

Dear God,

When I lift up my eyes unto the hills and watch the place where the sky meets the mountains' crest, waiting for your help to come into view, my hands shake.

To the One who made heaven and earth, my problems are the size of dust, but dust clouds vision, causes eyes to water, and sojourners to lose their way as they cross the desert en route to the Promised Land.

I've walked so long with your cloud guiding me by day and your fire by night.

I know you didn't bring me into the desert to die. I no longer dream of the seductive, poisonous comforts of Egypt, but I stand here, at the Jordan, watching the river's quick churning current, and it's not drowning that scares me the most.

Who will I be once I live in your promise? Who am I when I'm not wandering? Struggling?

I don't know how to live, only to survive, and this river wants to give me a new hope and a new name that feels unfamiliar on my lips.

I need you more than ever as I walk into this place.

Please take my hand. Don't let me fall.

Love,
Me

Dear God,

My Father, who art in heaven. Who led me through night forests full of hungry, howling monsters. Who walked with me through barren deserts of despair. Who fought invisible armies while I cried, huddled, and called your name.

Who never left me, not for one moment. Who knows my heart better than I do and cherishes it. Who dries my tears and restores the burned ruins of my hope.

Who taught me how to love by loving me before I knew your name.

Thank you.

I love you. Now and forever. Brokenly and in your wholeness.

Love,
Me

DEAR GOD,

On the days I can't remember who I am—when my name is sullied beyond repair by my own standards, confused—I try to remember who you are.

And then the thought comes: What if I've made you up? What if, in my desperation for someone to love me despite my repeated failings, to absolve me of all I've done wrong, what if I drew you out of the smoke rising out of the ashes of my dreams?

But no. Even if the miracles I've seen were all hallucinations, blessings, luck, interventions, coincidences, even if grace is a gentle mental mechanism, you're far too beautiful for me to have created. I could have never.

Nothing I've been told about you, nothing I've learned about you, has come close to the untouchable, unimaginable beauty that is feeling your soft, sweet, holy, and majestic presence—and none of it was of my design.

So you're real. And here. With me. Not as vapor merely exists above a quiet lake at dawn, but here by your own choice. Being with me.

Help me to feel you. Help me to be still and know that you are God. You are the one thing in life I cannot, I will not, live without.

Love,
ME

DEAR GOD,

Thank you for the people who care. Thank you for the ones who see a need and rise. Thank you for the tender hearts, the ones who sweeten the oft-bitter tea of life.

Thank you for the ones who sit by those who sit alone, despite multiple invitations to packed tables.

Thank you for the ones who ask, "How are you?" and look you in the eye, waiting for the truth, and who are ready, with compassionate words, to wrap gauze around the scrapes from life's recent blows.

Thank you for the ones who hold the trembling hands of the outcasts and meet them where they are.

Thank you for the ones who draw lines in the sand and stand up against mobs holding stones.

Thank you for those who give you half of their sandwich, even when it's your own fault for leaving lunch at home.

Thank you for those who feed stomachs before minds, give hugs before teachings, and help pull you out of the fire before the reprimand for playing with matches.

Help me to be one. Help me to love.

Love,
ME

DEAR GOD,

Purify my heart. Stir my soul and let the thick steam that rises from it warm those around me. Keep me tender but resilient. Be my strength and flood my thoughts.

I want your love to flow through my hands and my mouth by day, and I want to hide within the cavern of your heart by night.

I beg you to sit with me beside the fire, the only light in the dark woods of this life. Until I realize, looking into the flames that don't burn, that you are the fire.

You are close to the brokenhearted and save those who are crushed in spirit.*

You promised that one day I'll soar like an eagle, whether in this life or the next.**

In the meantime, be the air I breathe, and let me lean against you and close my eyes.

Love,
ME

---

*   See Psalm 34:18.
** See Isaiah 40:31.

DEAR GOD,

The secret hurt I hold on to, the one I use as a shield to protect myself from rain, I know it also blocks out the sun.

It's jagged, sharp, and heavy, so heavy.

But I need it. So rather than cast it into the ocean where it may sink into the unknown, my memories still attached, can you hold it for me?

In the same way a small child hands her mother or father a shiny pebble or a small tree branch for safekeeping on a long walk home, I give it to you.

I know you'll take care of it.

So I can walk easier for a little bit.

Thank you, Abba, for your infinite pockets.

Love,
ME

Dear God,

Thank you for the butterscotch and crimson maple leaves of fall.

Thank you for a warm, soft, familiar bed to sink into every night.

Thank you for the crisp, grapefruit pink sunrise of early morning and apricot marmalade sunsets of evening.

Thank you for holding body and soul together through uncertain nights and days spotted with hazards unknown.

Thank you for rivers of your love's remembrance I can sit by anytime, soaking my heart in yours whenever hope begins to dry up.

*This life feels short, long, then short again. Joy makes days lurch forward, pain stretches hours into months, but through it all, you are my shepherd. Your rod and your staff, they comfort me.**

Love,
Me

---

* See Psalm 23.

DEAR GOD,

Please bless the broken. Please lay heaven's kiss on the hidden damage and cleanse the deepest wounds. Please breathe healing over scraped hands and trembling hearts. Please pick up your crying babies and whisper, "There, there," tapping their backs until sobs calm into steady breathing against your embrace.

Hold us, Abba. Don't let us go. Ever. You promised. I love you. We need you.

Love,
ME

Dear God,

Thank you for the sound of raindrops falling against wet sidewalks.

Thank you for the way a good hug can melt loneliness out of my bones.

Thank you for the smell of freshly baked bread, hot out of the oven.

Thank you for kittens.

Thank you for checks that show up right on time.

Thank you for how a long sip of cool water tastes.

Thank you for friendly dogs' thick, soft coats.

Thank you for small dogs with big attitudes.

Thank you for the snowflakes that seem to fall in slow motion.

Thank you for friends who know just when to call.

Thank you for angels who nudge us this way and that.

Thank you for peace that defies circumstances, your invisible umbrella of grace.

Thank you for loving me on my worst days.

Thank you for being you.

Love,
Me

Dear God,

Thank you for pomegranates—a fruit and a puzzle all in one.

Thank you for kitten paws.

Thank you for candles and their soft, golden, flickering light.

Thank you for meadows. Thank you for wildflowers and their reminder that not everything beautiful has to be fancy.

Thank you for baby giggles, the way they squeak and chortle in uncontrollable, hilarious gasps of delight.

Thank you for gentle people, earth angels, who walk amongst us, doing no harm.

Thank you for the soft, thin skin of an elderly palm.

Thank you for filling my heart when I need it most.

Thank you for knowing me by name.

Thank you for counting the hairs on my head and catching each tear.

Thank you for watching me sleep and waking me up when I need to talk.

Thank you for making me yours.

Thank you for being mine.

Love,
Me

DEAR GOD,

You brought me here for a reason. I know that. You're not a God of mistakes or accidents.

You formed me with your hands.

I feel out of place here. I don't fit in. I'm often alone, even when surrounded, but because I know who I am to you, I can get through.

My prayer today is that whatever you created me for, I will do it. When I embrace the blinding light, I want—no, I yearn, I crave—to hear you say, "Well done, my child."

I'm not pretending to do any of this perfectly or even well. But you can see what no one else can—this broken heart that beats only for you.

I heard a song once: "And the things of earth will grow strangely dim, in the light of his glory and grace."*

You are it for me. My true love.

Show me your fingerprints on my soul.

Love,
ME

---

* Helen H. Lemmel, "Turn Your Eyes upon Jesus" (1922). Public domain.

Dear God,

Today the dam broke. I felt nothing at first as I watched the floodwaters destroy the future I'd created in my imagination, drown it in its merciless, powerful waves.

My body went cold and unmoving as everything on which I'd hinged my prayers and worth became floating debris.

When my mind began working again, my first thought was that you are not real.

You couldn't be.

No loving God, no powerful, loving God, would let this happen, allow my life to be stomped into a crime scene after all I've already survived.

As the world rocked under my feet and my heart screamed in silent pain, it seemed preferable that you not exist at all rather than exist and allow this day.

But in the chaos, your heartiest angel bravely—and I say bravely because if I could have swatted it like a mosquito, I would have—whispered reminders of the glittering miracles I've seen with my own eyes and touched with my own hands.

And my angel assigned to me from before birth somewhere eternal, showed me bodies of those you've loved who exited this world in degrading, terrible ways.

I don't know the why, but I trust you will show me one day.

And tonight, as I lie in my soft bed, cried-out and tired, I can say the words of Horatio Spafford as he stared into the ocean that swallowed his four beloved daughters' hearts: It is well with my soul.*

I can't speak for my mind.

My body has scars.

But my soul, the waters so deep only you can stir them, is still.

Hold me close, now and forever, Father.

Love,
ME

---

* Horatio G. Spafford, "It Is Well with My Soul" (1873). Public domain.

DEAR GOD,

I'm in bed now. The day is over. Thank you for seeing me through. I am ragged in some places, bone-tired, but we made it. Your grace was sufficient for me. Thank you. Please pour your Spirit over me, mine, and ours again tomorrow. I can't do it without you.

Love,
ME

On the days hope feels like a cruel mirage,
when you're wandering,
spinning in place,
unable to believe there are plans to prosper and not
      harm you,
unable to believe there are any good plans with your
      name on them,
listen.
Hope does not exist to make fools out of pilgrims,
for when it is placed in the hands of the eternal,
it is the scent of things to come.
Let go of your imaginings of what life is meant to look
      like
and let hope lift your soul up and away from present
      pains,
providing respite
and breath enough
for one more step forward.

DEAR GOD,

Why do you like to talk to me at night? Is it because I'm at my most still, the jumpiest parts of myself quieted by fatigue? At night, when my mind is three-quarters asleep, you whisper love and comfort into my ears and bathe my heart in peace.

You are unwilling to compete with the noise of the day. The noise behind my eyes. So you wait. Until I've laid down my broken tools and am a child—mask off, curled up in warm, soft pajamas, drifting off to dreamland. You sit by my bed and remind me that no matter what I see, all is well.

Thank you for loving me. I'll try to listen when the sun is out too.

Love,
ME

DEAR GOD,

Please forgive me for my mistakes.

Sometimes I try to clean them up or cover them with a soiled cloth, but I am incapable of doing either.

I forget that you're the healer, the fixer, the redeemer,

and I try to be the janitor,

dragging a dirty mop through gray water,

moving the mess around,

cleansing nothing.

Forgive me, God.

Please forgive my mistakes, my pride, my forgetfulness, my shame.

I'm yours.

Love,
ME

Dear God,

The world is on fire. It seems evil men are the ones with all the power and keys. All of the beauty you created—we've poisoned it, mining out the heart of it, never stopping, our greed and desire insatiable. Abba, I'm sorry. Please forgive us. Help us.

Please send angels to cleanse what we've muddied, restore what we've broken, and let your justice finally come down like a hammer of light. Please hear the cries of the innocent. I know you do. Please wrap them in your blanket tonight. Protect them from the cold. Whether shivering from frost or loneliness. Please wrap them. Please feed them. Please show me how to be your hand, your voice, your kindness.

I'm overwhelmed by our mess.

But you're not.

Help me to be something other than a parasite to your creation.

Love,
Me

DEAR GOD,

Somewhere, someone is crying. On edge. About to let go. Shaking, aching, fingers tired of gripping what hurts and ready to take a final breath and let go, sink downward into the black waters.

God, please send an angel of light to take their hands. Let despair part and hope rise in their heart. Let them not just see dawn but feel it. Let them find rest in a promise known only to you and them.

Rescue them, please.

Like you rescued me.

Love,
ME

Dear God,

I'm seeing it now. All this pain. It's helped me to love more like you do.

Don't let me go. Don't drop my hand. I'll wander off. We both know it.

Keep me close.

Love,
Me

Dear God,

I'm up and awake. Nervously scrolling through pages of today's to-do list. The light of the moon glows white behind my window in the dark, but I know the sun will soon yawn awake.

I'm afraid. Inside the body driving to and fro in stop-and-go traffic, behind the face making pleasant small talk— laughing softly at all the right times, mouth pulled into a bright smile, at the helm of the hands deciding which order to break the boulders that keep rolling toward me each day, the tasks that never stop—is a trembling child.

I have no doubt that I can finish what needs to be done. Or most of it. I can throw small buckets of water on the most pressing fires while apologizing for all the smoke. As for the blaze raging in the distance, creeping slowly closer to me daily, I push it out of my mind, imagining that angels dressed in dew will tame the flames into lit candles.

But even if I do everything all right today, get a B-, what is this doing to me? I'm so tired at the end of each day. I sink into my bed, exhausted. I'm worried the gasoline I'm running on is made from my bones, my own fossil fuel. Unsustainable. Dangerous.

Adam was cursed to till the earth. Eve to bear children. And me to do both?

I know I am blessed. I know I live with blessings some pray for with tear-streaked faces, and I am grateful.

But I am tired.

So I pray not for escape, because there is nowhere to go. Not for more help or friends.

I pray for grace. Let me run on you for a few miles. For the whole day. For my whole life. Continually refresh my spirit and body, please. Breathe fresh air into my lungs and tranquility into my heart when I'm scared.

Remember me. Your baby. Keep your eye on me and don't look away.

Bathe me in grace. Submerge me. I can breathe there.

I love you.

Let's go.

Love,
ME

DEAR GOD,

I often wonder why you didn't give us gills. And I know it's because if we could breathe underwater, we'd stay there.

We were meant to live on dry land. Help me find a shore where I can lie down, back on hot, sandy earth, and warm up under the hot sun.

Love,
ME

DEAR GOD,

I like you. I like how when I know I've come tragically short in life, when I lie in bed disgusted with what I couldn't do and who I couldn't be, there you are.

Still here.

Sitting by my bed, holding up a garment, one so much better than I deserve but mine all the same.

I wrap it around myself and it runs over the thorns in my flesh, not catching or snagging but smoothing and soothing. How does it do that? This garment—it's not silk or cotton, no, it's heavenly. It's my identity in you. The one I curl up in when this world, or my riddled mind, tries to give me a new name.

I only have one name. The one you gave me. Maybe I don't live up to it every day but it's still mine and it echoes in the chamber of my soul, a chant birthed by your breath, and I am sustained.

No day can take away what you've given me. No day can take away my name.

Yours, forever.

Love,
ME

Dear God,

*Sometimes this life feels like a game of hide-and-seek.
You hiding amongst the clouds while I, your child, hunt.
Giggling as you move about, leading me closer and
closer . . . to what?*

Your kingdom? My destiny?

*On the days the sun shines bright and clear, I revel in
our game, laugh loudly, sing even louder, and your own
laughter erupts—thunder cracking in the mountains.*

*On days the winds are too strong, I lose your scent and
become afraid. I crouch in the tall grass, hands over my
face, and weep until you find me, wipe my tears, and help
me stand on shaky legs.*

*On the days it rains—oh, you know how I love the rain—
when it pours, I tilt my chin toward the sky and thank you
for giving nature the ability to cry with us.*

*Between games, your arms are around me, and I know this
is all for me. For us. You're leading us home, aren't you?*

Ready or not, here I come.

Love,
Me

DEAR GOD,

You gave me a friend today. She walks on four legs and is covered in hair. She's also a bit needy. Cries a lot. Remind you of anyone?

Thank you for dogs.

From the bottom of my heart, thank you.

I was nervous; I'm not going to lie. It seems like I can barely take care of myself these days, but I don't know. Every time she looks at me, begging for a head scratch, flipping her enormous head into my lap as if we've known each other all our lives, something inside me gets reconnected.

I don't feel so alone.

She likes hugs, which is good. I can't leave her for more than ten seconds or she starts wailing, weeping quite loudly. I know how you must feel now. But it's nice.

I get the sense she'd walk miles by my side in a blizzard, and I haven't even found her a proper food bowl yet.

Is that why you created dogs? To remind us of how pure love and loyalty can be if we let it?

She's a masterpiece.

How do I get her to listen?

Thank you.

Thank you.

Thank you.

Love,
ME

Dear God,

Today I got a glimpse of a new season. A better one, and I was afraid.

I guess somewhere in these back-to-back hard days, I started to believe the storm was my destiny.

Who will I be when I'm not treading water? Who will I be when I'm not struggling?

If my name is not Hardship, what is it?

And . . . will we be this close?

What frightened me the most is that when I saw those first peach and daffodil rays of dawn, my desperate grip on you, my life preserver in the stilling waters, began to loosen.

Who will you be to me when I walk in new light? Am I even able to do anything but survive?

And as the fears began to rise, you gently walked me through them, banishing them to the left and right. You are life, not death. You aren't the darkness; you entered it to find me.

We will be fine in all seasons, won't we? You're not going anywhere. Promise me again like you always do.

Even if I could survive without you, I wouldn't want to.

Hold my hand for life, and beyond.

Love,
Me

DEAR GOD,

I wasn't there when you laid the foundations of the earth, breathed directions to the winds, or gave each star a name.*

My questioning you is as ludicrous as paint screaming at the painter, but I have to know why. Why all of this? Pain and struggle? Death and injustice? At every turn, evil waves a flag of victory, it seems.

We're tired. I'm tired. I'm afraid of what will come.

You promised life more abundantly, and while there are ribbons of peace and joy, this gift of life is often one I want to return.

I know you're here with me, but it's only barely enough to survive. I'm tired of being handed just enough of your manna, your grace and presence, for one day. Give me more than my daily bread; I want my feast.

But it's not time. So I stumble through this race, barely seeing the path ahead through a blur of tears—sometimes from pain, sometimes from laughter at the craziness of all of this.

Don't be angry at me when I sit down from time to time, Abba. It's hard, and I'm weak. I told you once, "I can't do this," and you said, "I know." With you, I can. Carry me. Carry us.

Love,
ME

---

* See Job 38:4; 28:25; Psalm 147:4.

Dear God,

*Someone once said everything happens for a reason.
I know that's not true. Not every tragedy has your
fingerprint on it.*

But you do see all.

*And you find us. In the dark. Weeping over our dead
dreams and loved ones.*

*You take what this world broke, gently prying the ashes
from our hands, and slowly lead us to still waters.**

*I don't believe you cause every storm, but you plant flowers
under our feet as we walk through them so that when your
sun finally does peek out from behind the clouds, something
blooms.*

Thank you. Help us.

Love,
Me

DEAR GOD,

Thank you for healing me. As you continue to stitch my heart together, please use forgiveness as the thread so that I stay soft. Wiser, but still soft enough to love the way you've loved me.

I've put myself back together in the past, stitched myself up crudely with other, lesser threads—unrelenting anger, self-righteousness, and hate solidified. Eventually, those threads rot, grow putrid, and the bitterness I believed would protect me spreads, infecting my mind, body, and spirit.

Abba, use your golden thread. The one with flecks of pearl and light. Cleanse my wounds with your kiss and seal them. I don't mind a small scar. It's how those who need you will find me. So I can tell them who the Healer is.

Thank you.

Love,
ME

DEAR GOD,

When you demand obedience in the storm, I assume it's because you want me to drown. I flail and scream, feeling icy waters like a million arctic hands pull me under, choke out my breath, and my lungs burn. And you ask, in that calm whisper, for obedience? While wave after crushing wave beats me into the sea, causing my feet, desperate for solid ground, to dash against sharp rocks? Obedience? As I struggle in the blackness of the waters, turning around and around, tossed by unforgiving riptides, wishing only to know which way is up? Obedience?

Yes, you say. And it's only because I know who you are—because you're all I have left—that I exhale my last breath. And let the stones I've turned to bread fall from my clenched hands.

ME

Dear God,

Everything you give me turns to dust in my hands, so I no longer ask for answers. Only peace. Your will be done. The safety of my loved ones. Their peace. Peace can survive. Peace is the rat after the apocalypse. The cockroaches after the blazing house. I sit in the rubble of my dreams and ask for peace alone.

Me

Dear God,

My siblings—the ones who believe—they frighten me.
They're afraid to love like you do. It's like they've never
tasted your grace, because if they had, wouldn't they offer a
drop of it to others?

They're afraid to lead with love. They call love a meal of
milk when meat is required, but what they mean is that
they don't want to offer hugs when they think lashes are
deserved.

It's just me and you, because I feel scared around them. I
couldn't let them hurt me again, so I ran.

They pretend to want me back, but what they want is my
body in the seat, another member to fill in the row. They
don't want my pain, my past, my mistakes, or my anger—
they don't want me.

They want a monthly check, someone to bring potato
salad. They don't want me.

I read somewhere that fitting in is what you do to gain
acceptance, but belonging is what you can be around
family. I'm tired of fitting in—squeezing and cutting off
the unacceptable parts of myself like a butcher with an
untrimmed piece of unkosher meat, salting and slicing until
I can pass for "good enough" for your children. So I am
alone with you.

It's quiet. The only sound is my soft crying.

But you're here, so I'm okay.

I still want to know though. Where is this "family" you promised?

Love,
Me

DEAR GOD,

What do I do when forgiveness feels impossible? My brain remembers all the times your grace has saved my life. But my heart—it's full of hatred, anger, and malice, the smoke offering from pain set on fire.

I cringe knowing the scent fills your nostrils. The smell of what I'm holding on to, letting it decay in my hands, chewing it over and over, unable to swallow, unable to spit. I've tried. I want to. I'm trying. It keeps coming back. All the memories.

I want to be free.

"Pray for them," you tell me, and I laugh.

I can't.

I pause and feel the words already forming from the piece of your pure Spirit that somehow lives within my dark cabin of a heart.

Your will and love swirl in pastels around me, beams of light causing the rancor to melt.

And then as I think the words, unable to say them aloud— Bless them—the oppression lifts. The crushing weight of it evaporates and blows away like a single layer of snow.

Exhausted gratitude is all I'm left with. For now. I know it'll come back. Tomorrow. Next week. Next month.

Remind me. Be patient with me. I'm trying.

Don't leave.

Love,
ME

Dear visitor,
Faith is not a country club.
There is no entrance fee,
no political party,
no uniform.
You'll know us by our love,
our sheepish apologies,
our desire for justice.
Forgive us for our failures.
Forgive us for the ones who
lead with hate and hypocrisy.
We're not perfect,
but we're trying,
striving,
falling and getting up,
not by our own strength
but by the One who called us here.
Welcome.

DEAR GOD,

All have sinned, but not all make a sport, game, business, out of rebreaking the broken. I expect violence from the world, but your house is a place of horrors. It is soaked in the blood of the ignored. Blind eyes take the place of knives. Harsh words pierce deeper than bullets, and the wounded stagger, bleeding, out the door, whispers whipping them as they leave.

Why would I go there? Why? The most harmless of sheep in your pasture gather together to protect the wolves. They offer up their lambs for lunch and praises for dinner.

Why would I go there? Why, when I can find you in the forest? You, unfiltered and untouched, unpolluted by men with agendas and women to protect them at all costs, why would I go there?

I'm staying home where no one can hurt me.

Love,
ME

Dear God,

I love you because you loved me first. You loved me at a time I thought myself unlovable. You loved me in a way that was both soft and fierce. You rescued me. And like anyone who has been rescued, pulled from the pit by a hand they thought would never come, I will love you forever. Because you first loved me.

Love,
Me

Dear God,

Some days, I wonder who I'd be if I'd had an easier life. But it was in the darkness that I turned to you. It was at my lowest when I first heard your voice. I know you are the author of joy and peace, but it was in the valley that you showed me the perfection of your love for me. So while I have no desire to go back, I can never hate that place.

Love,
Me

Dear God,

I know your children, not by their declarations of faith,
memorization of Scripture, or the size or shape of their
impressive buildings, but by their love. Love is the
fingerprint that binds us. It's the undeniable scent of
you that follows yours. It sparkles in gentle eyes. It turns
strangers into my family. Your love transforms anger into
still lakes and pain into doves. Your love sustains and is
generous. Your love is the most beautiful treasure I've ever
known. I'd know it anywhere.

Love,
Me

DEAR GOD,

What does it mean to lift up my eyes?* To me, it means
looking just above, where the sky kisses the mountain peak,
the place where the prophets met with you to ask for help.
Sometimes I get so transfixed by what's happening, I forget
who rules heaven and earth. God, Father, when the battle
is terrifying and mesmerizing, when I can barely tear my
gaze away, help me, remind me, to look up.

ME

---

* See Psalms 121; 123.

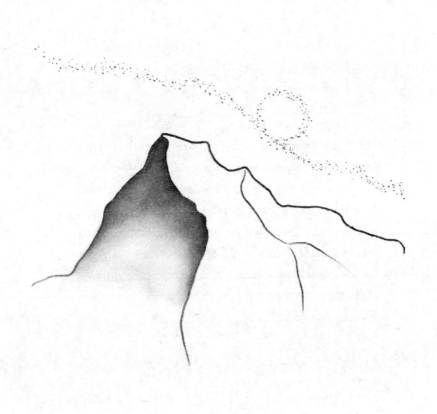

Dear God,

What is holiness? Something so pure and perfect. Set apart. And yet you walked into my dingy, infested reality, my crumbling, blood-soaked crime scene of an existence, teeming with decades of garbage made into coping mechanisms. You picked up my infected, tattered heart and kissed it. Kissed it. I still don't understand why. But knowing you stepped down from your pristine throne to claim me as your own . . . my life is yours. I am yours. Forever. My heart belongs to you.

Me

DEAR GOD,

Faith is such a short, gentle word to describe what is a warm, thick cloak that when wrapped in takes the sting out of the harshest winds of change. It's a glittering shield to protect against the attacks of doubt and how things look through human eyes. It's a machete to chop through dense jungle, hacking at ropy vines as we walk unexplored lands.

It gives us the strength to love when a lesser action would suffice.

Faith is a way of being, yes, but it's also a choice you lead me to make, sometimes daily but more often, moment by shaking breath moment.

Thank you for the gift of faith.

Love,
ME

Dear God,

I asked you why. Why did you plant the tree in the garden?
And you asked me why I chose knowledge over innocence.

Innocence? Innocence in the presence of a choice is no
longer innocence but chosen ignorance, I told you, a
scared finger pointing. I know the angels must shudder as I
dare point a finger at the One they've seen fling stars into
the sky.

But innocence? Innocence is only innocence when it's not
a choice. That's the beauty of it in its natural state. Did
you not remove my innocence simply by dangling a choice
before me?

Yes, I chose knowledge over obedience. I will own that. But
not over innocence. Once the truth of the tree was known,
did my innocence not evaporate into morning fog?

But you knew this, didn't you? You knew how I'd choose,
even when warning me not to. Why? Not to trap me. I
know you enough by now.

So why?

And you showed me. How one can only know a thing by
experiencing the other. How black is known because of
white. And how spring is anticipated, known, and craved
only after a long winter.

Sweet is enjoyed because we know bitterness.

You knew that once the choice to know was given, we

would choose to know, the same way a toddler reaches for a flame.

We return to you, singed but wiser, ready to trade our knowledge for your arms once again. Haggard and scarred from battles fought—some lost, but the war won—we are children once more.

Because you wanted your love to be a choice we made, not a blind obligation.

You waited, heavyhearted and missing us, for our yes.

You have it now—my yes.

I'm yours.

I'm home.

I choose you.

ME

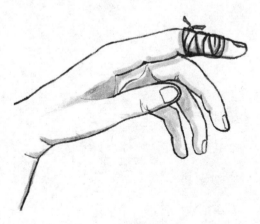

Dear saints,

One day,
life on earth will be a distant memory,
a hazy remembrance
of days past,
a story in an old book
on a high shelf.
Our every day will be heaven.
Sparkling gems, our pebbles,
the glory, our breath.
The battle will be long over—
make it count.
Push.

Love,
BUNMI

Acknowledgments

Thank you to my mother and father for making it a priority to teach me about God.

Thank you to my children— M, T, and F—for their love, their joy, and, most importantly, their laughter.

Thank you to Esther for showing me what strength and sisterhood looks like.

Thank you to Jenny for being my kindest, gentlest friend.

Thank you to Austin for seeing me and liking me anyway.

Thank you to Elizabeth for taking me in.

Thank you to Anna for being my twin for life.

Thank you to Helen for being my family.

Thank you to Holly for seeing something in me.

Thank you to Carolyn for believing enough for the both of us.

Thank you to Zondervan for taking a chance on me.

Thank you to God for never letting me go.